SILLIEST VERSE IN THE UNIVERSE

BY LUKE MILLER

ISBN: 9781730995538

Independently published (2018)

THAT CERTAIN CAT BOOKS

For my kids who also like silly verse ;)

CONTENTS

According to the local zoo 4
Are we nearly there yet? 5
At the park 6
Strange words 7
Brad the robot 8
Bring me food 9
Creepy crawlies on the loose 10
Daddy has a poorly toe 11
Egg Rolling 12
It's snowing 13
Want 14
Last night 15
Lois Lois 16
Marching ants night 17
Millionaires next door 18
Monster makes a terrible noise 19
Moose on the loose 20
Mummy cuddles, muddy puddles 21
Peas 22
Peculiar Julia 23
Poor Old Louis 24
Peculiar Julia 25
Pyjamas 26
Raincatcher 27
Run to the hills 28
Silly Old Troll 29
Smelly Socks 30
Space Mice 31
Special Teddy 32
Steggie 33
The furbulous four 34
The fuller figure 35
The little boy who didn't like anything 36
The dreams of a mermaid 37
Thunderstorms 38

Tickle Me 39
Uncle Ben 40
When I grow up I want to be a vet 41
When baths attack 42
Where did all these cats come from? 43
Yeti 44
Without 45
These poems are atrocious 46

Page 3

According to the local zoo

According to the local zoo
We all should remain calm
But yesterday something escaped
Thus raising the alarm
It wasn't the orangutans
The pelicans or bisen
The zoo has only gone and lost
Their twelve foot burmese python

Someone left the door open
A truly big mistake
Now there's pandemonium
The python has escaped
The python is called "Caroline"
She's actually quite new
And came from Southern Florida
Before she joined the zoo

So everyone tread carefully
Keep looking at your feet
Caroline is hiding
And in need of things to eat
She also might be up a tree
Or hiding in some water
Can we truly breathe again
Until someone has caught her?

Are we nearly there yet?

Are we nearly there yet?
They ask as Dad starts driving
No, we're off to Scotland kids
I'll say when we're arriving

Now we need a wee they cry
We've barely just begun
You should've gone before we left
Now listen everyone

I don't want you fighting
No elbowing no thrashing
The driver has to concentrate
Or else we'll end up crashing

Can we stop, it's really hot
My finger needs a plaster
Mummy, can I have a sweet
Dad, can we go faster?

Nausea seeps through the car
And suddenly it's silent
"Mummy I don't feel too well"
We brace for something *violent*

On the dual carriageway
Nearly there at last
I think we left the oven on
We're heading back home fast

At the park

At the park there's always lots of
things to see and do
There's swings to swing on
Slides to slide down
Fun for me and you

Ducks and geese and fish to feed
A train goes round the lake
A cafe which has won awards
Sells ice cream, drinks and cake

A bandstand which has been
restored
The annual dog show!
We go there at the weekends
It's a perfect place to go

We live quite near, it only takes a
minute to get to
 At the park there's always lots of
things to see and do

Strange words

Bilbble, blabble, bift and boften
These are words you don't hear often
Used instead when all words fail
Used to get you out of jail?

Don't pass go and don't collect
With curious words, be circumspect
Words can send you down an alley
Send you utterly doolally

Bilbble, blabble, bift and boften
These are words you don't hear often

Brad the robot

Edward built a robot
From lots of bit and bobs
He called it Brad
And showed his Dad
Who gave it lots of jobs

Like tidying the garden
And pulling up the weeds
Brad did the lot
And for it got
A sticker for good deeds

Poor Brad he soon got hungry
He had to eat some metal
He zoomed around
And soon he found
And ate a rusty kettle

Bring me food

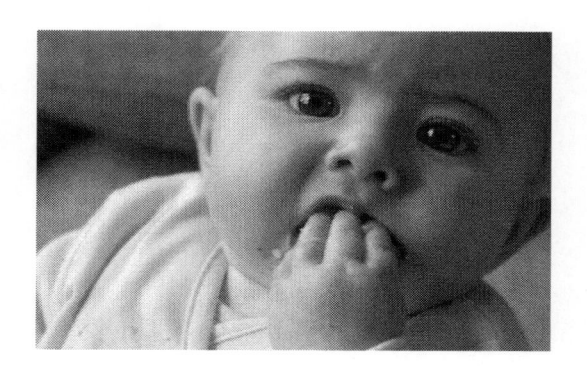

Rose, Boze sits up to the table
"Bring me food" she cries
She bangs her spoon
And rocks her chair
She throws her dinner everywhere

The 'cleaners' down on hands and knees
Tidy up all day
"I think we need a brand new carpet
This one's had its day"

Creepy crawlies on the loose

My sister likes her insects
She likes them big and small
She potters around the garden
Looking for them all

She puts them all together
In a big glass jar
She brought them in
And lost the lid
Now who knows where they are!?

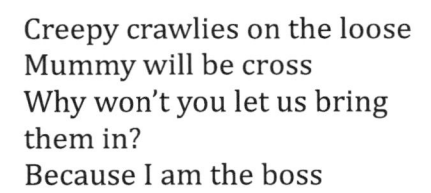

Creepy crawlies on the loose
Mummy will be cross
Why won't you let us bring them in?
Because I am the boss

Now, Spiders on the sofa
Snails up on the ceiling
Woodlice underneath the chairs
This isn't too appealing

Daddy has a poorly toe

Daddy has a poorly toe
How he got it we don't know
But yesterday he made a noise
Falling on a pile of toys
It must've hurt
It made him cry
This might be the reason why
Daddy has a poorly toe

Egg Rolling

Have you ever been egg rolling?
It's simple and it's brill
All you need to do
Is find a decent hill

Everybody takes an egg
They decorate it nice
Then off we march with eggs in hand
To start the egg roll race

Standing at the hilltop
Waiting to begin
A line of fancy painted eggs
I wonder who will win?

You're not allowed to throw it
Your egg has to be rolled
The winner is the one who's egg
Goes furthest so I'm told

It's snowing

Look out the window it's snowing!
School is closed so won't be going!
Instead we can go
And play out in the snow
But we'll wrap up
The North Wind is blowing

Want

I want to run on open beaches
Only want to eat tinned peaches

Want to fly on a dragon's back
Want a peek in Santa's sack

Want to ride inside his sleigh
Want a birthday every day

Never want to have to wait
Want to stay up really late

Want to be a millionaire
Want to have Kate Middleton's hair

Want to live inside a palace
Want to change my name to Alice

Want my Dad to be Darth Vader
 Want a go with his light sabre

People say don't be so greedy
I can't help it if I'm needy

Last night

Last night I had a funny dream
I ate a centipede ice cream
We had a party on a cloud
With only butterflies allowed
I caught a passing hot air balloon
Driven by a green baboon
He dropped me off in time for tea
Right in the middle of the sea

Lois Lois

Lois, Lois, accident prone
Fell off a bed and broke a bone

Lois, Lois, isn't she brave?
Though sometimes known to misbehave

Lois, Lois, an 'eating machine'
You just can't seem to keep her clean

Lois, Lois, lovely girl
Cheekiest one in the whole wide world

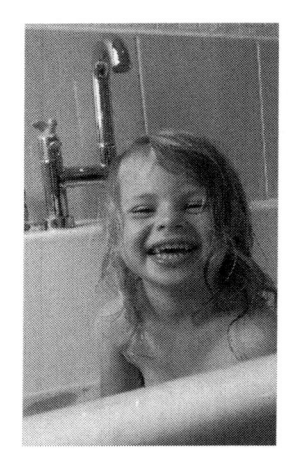

Marching ants night

Look at these marching ants
Marching across the page
Leaving muddy footprints too
This is an OUTRAGE!

Millionaires next door

Our neighbours won the lottery
Though nothing's changed it seems
They won the super jackpot
Rich beyond their wildest dreams

Then money started oozing
from their letter box and windows
And coins would fly out of their chimneys
Like fiery cash volcanoes

With sports cars sitting In the drive
A swimming pool, brand new
With all this new found money
They did not know what to do

In the end their winnings
Started getting in the way
So Mr Roberts and his wife
Just gave it all away

Monster makes a terrible noise

Monster makes a terrible noise
Monster eats a small boy's toys
Monster just won't go away
Monster sleeps throughout the day

Monster has a purple tail
Monster checks his googlemail
Monster hides below my bed
Monster lives inside my head

Moose on the loose

There's a moose on the loose, so be careful
He's galloping around like a loon
And singing rude words
It's scaring the birds
He's not even singing in tune!

Mummy cuddles, muddy puddles

Massive, squeezy, Mummy cuddles
Make me feel like rhubarb crumble
I can have them any time
Have them even when I'm nine

Massive, mucky, muddy puddles
Help me turn my trousers brown
I jump in with not a care
It doesn't matter what I wear

Peas

Odd, odd, peas in a pod
Peas in the freezer
Eaten by Louisa
Green and round
Roll on the ground
Under the table
Reach if you're able

Peas on a plate
Yummy in the tummy
Grown from a seed in the soil by Mummy

Peculiar Julia

Peculiar Julia,
Odd little toddler
Shes looks quite strange
But I still want to cuddle her

Eyes like jewels
Big and round
A tiny little mouth
That never makes a sound

Nobody's ever heard her cry
She likes to poke you in the eye

"She's incredibly intelligent"
Confesses her Mum
As Julia sits there sucking her thumb

Peculiar Julia
Is growing up fast
She did her A-levels early
And passed

Poor Old Louis

Poor old Louis
'Family cat'
Used to get a stroke
Used to get a pat
Used to lie and sleep in the sun all day long
But three things happened and it went all wrong

First came Wendy.
She made lots of noise
She stroked him using assorted toys

Just as this was beginning to stop
Along came Ralph with his 'belly flop'

Then came Edith
Full of affection
But she stroked his fur in the wrong direction

Louis somehow made it through.
He didn't lose his wits
Now they stroke him gently whilst he munches cat biscuits

Poodle doodle diddle bod

Poodle doodle, diddle bod
Ooky, mooky, nooky noo
Acky, tocky, ticky tat
Bing bong boo

Liffle, piffle, paffle pat
Puggy, tiggy, soggy chee,
Magga,lagga, cush cosh
Bang, Ding Dee

Ickle,tackle,tockle tang
Fangy wang wing
Wip,wop,wapple snap
Abba dabba ding

Pyjamas

I love my pyjamas
I know this might sound wrong
But if I had my own way I would wear them all day long

And now it's getting funny
And you might even laugh
But I wear my pyjamas when I'm sitting in the bath

Raincatcher

What do you do if you're stuck in the rain
Without a hat or a coat?
Tilt your head back
Open your mouth
And catch all the drops in your throat

Run to the hills

Run to the hills
Run to the hills
Run to the valleys and streams
There's a troll on his way
He's tired and grumpy
His porridge this morning was cold and lumpy
He needs a rest (He needs a bath!)
He needs a plate of food
Hide your goats
Hide your puddings
This troll can be terribly rude

Silly Old Troll

Look at this silly old troll
Lost in the middle of a wood
He knows not where he's going
I'd help him if I could

But trolls they do not listen
In one ear, out the other
Leave him be, let him find
His own way back to Mother

Smelly Socks

My brother has got smelly socks
His feet are the problem I think
He doesn't put them in the bath you see
And now they really stink

Space Mice

Some say the moon is made of cheese but me, I don't see how
If it was, the spacemice would have eaten it by now

Special Teddy

I have a little teddy bear that's special
He talks to me but no-one else can hear
You wouldn't know
He's very shy
I know you think
This is a lie
But 'special' teddy whispers in my ear

Steggie

When I was five, I got a special gift for my birthday
A dinosaur! Mummy had to get it on ebay

I wanted diplodocus but that one was too big for us
So instead we had to get a baby stegosaurus

But baby stegosauruses, they grow up rather quick
And when he caught the dinopox it made him very sick

We took him to the doctor who sent him to the vet
Looking back we should've got a rabbit for a pet

The furbulous four

Welcome oh ladies and gentlemen
I'd like you to give warm applause
The band is all ready to kick off the show
T his first one's called *Lovin' ya paws*

Harmonies swooping like angels
Melodies you can't ignore
This talented mouse, rabbit, kitten and dog
Are known as the furbulous four

The band is performing their last song
They hope you don't want an encore
You've heard all the songs that they're written
They simply don't have any more!

The fuller figure

My Dad's big but Mummy's bigger
She says "Dad likes a 'fuller' figure"
She puts on clothes and tries on shoes
The mirror rarely disapproves
The wardrobe mind, is full of stuff
Dad says "Don't you have enough?"

The little boy who didn't like anything

There was a little boy,
Who didn't like schools
He didn't like teachers
He didn't like rules
He didn't like playgrounds
He didn't like muck
He didn't like reading
He didn't like *this* book

The dreams of a mermaid

At the bottom of the sea is a seabed
In the bed is a pretty mermaid
She's dreaming of whales with elegant tails
Who serve her cold lemonade

Thunderstorms

I'm a fan of thunderstorms
To me, they are not frightening

I like it when the sky goes **boom** but
The best bit is the lightning

Tickle Me

* It wouldn't be the end of the world if the actions described within this poem were reenacted on any nearby listeners

I like being tickled
Tickling is fun
Tickle underneath my arms
Tickle on my tum

Tickle me around my neck
Listen to me giggle
Tickle from a safe distance
It always make me wriggle

Tickle me behind the knees
And don't forget my toes
Tickle with a feather
Wave it underneath my nose

Tickle in the morning
Tickle late at night
And when we've finished tickling
Let's have a pillow fight!

Uncle Ben

Our Uncle *Ben* does not make rice
It doesn't stop him being nice
He works for Microsoft in the week
And doesn't mind being called a geek

When I grow up I want to be a vet

When I grow up I want to be a vet
That is all I really want to be
Helping poorly dogs and cats
And poorly guinea pigs and rats
Sounds like a perfect life indeed for me

When baths attack

We were having a bath
My sisters and I
When Daddy announced it's time to get dry
It's time to get out
He said scratching his beard
And this was when things became awfully weird

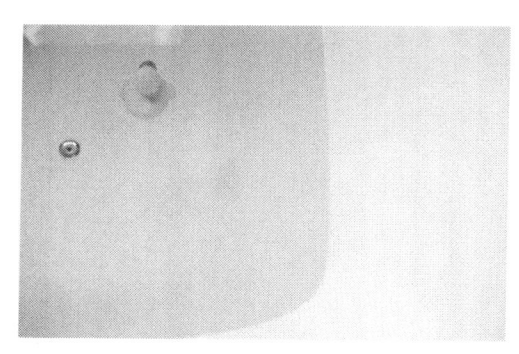

He went to fetch towels
But whilst he was gone
The plug hole had started to drink everyone
It first drank the water
And then all the toys
It was making a horrible gurgling noise

Me and my sisters
Were next to go down
When Dad raced back in with a shriek and a frown
He grabbed hold of Rosie
Who grabbed hold of me
And I clung on tightly to poor Emily

He pulled us out slowly
It took half an hour
Dad says in future we'll stick to the shower

Where did all these cats come from?

Where did all these cats come from?
I really cannot say
These furry beasts are everywhere
And getting in the way

Now I'm a great cat lover
Without them I'm alone
But surely there's a limit
To how many you can own?

Yeti

At the bottom of our garden lives a yeti
He's hairy and he likes to eat spaghetti
At night he walks around
Leaving footprints in the ground
As he listens to the music of Tom Petty

Without

What's a witch without a wand?
What's a frog without a pond?
What's a dog without a bark?
Where's a ghost without the dark?
What's a lion without a roar?
What's a room without a door?
What's a shark without a fin?
Where's the end with no begin?
What's the heart without some love?
Where's below with no above?
Where's the fire without a flame?
What's a thing without a name?
What's a bird without a beak?
What's a bum without a cheek?

Ignore all things upon this list
None of them in fact exist

These poems are atrocious

A friend of mine she said to me
Your poems are atrocious
Your writing style is very strange
Your manner quite precocious
Your rhymes I find them quite obscene
You really have no right
To publish them and make me read
them to my kids at night

I said to him that's fine my friend
Although it makes me sad
That you do not appreciate them
They are not *that* bad
Why don't you try them one more time
It's possible you'll find
That after reading one or two you
might just change your mind

THE END...

Printed in Poland
by Amazon Fulfillment
Poland Sp. z o.o., Wrocław